Starting Strong
In
Government
Contracting

*AN INTRODUCTION TO DOING BUSINESS WITH
FEDERAL, STATE, AND LOCAL GOVERNMENTS*

Steven T. Graff

Copyright © 2024 by

STEVEN T. GRAFF

Printed in the United States of America

Published by Authorssolution.com

TABLE OF CONTENTS

CHAPTER 1

GOVERNMENT PROCUREMENT UNVEILED

Embarking on the journey into the world of government contracting reveals a landscape rich with lucrative business opportunities that spread across all levels of governance, including city, county, state, and federal agencies. This book will dig deep into the complex and multifaceted world of government procurement, a vital component in the operation of a wide variety of agencies, departments, and entities covered under the blanket term "government."

Purchasing goods and services is a necessary part of any business, and the business of governing is no different. Government procurement operates on a massive scale, is governed by a complex framework of regulations, policies, and laws, and when done correctly, can be a profitable source of revenue for private businesses.

In this chapter, we begin our exploration of the intricacies of government procurement, unraveling the world of federal, state, and local entities and the unique challenges presented by each.

UNDERSTANDING FEDERAL AGENCIES

Government contracting centers around the huge number of federal agencies and their individual needs for products and services to successfully conduct the missions assigned to them. Digging deeper into government procurement requires understanding the role played by each agency, what their specific missions are, and how they are vital to the U.S. government.

As the largest agency, the DoD handles procurement related to national defense, from military hardware to support services for each branch of the military. Navigating DoD procurement requires understanding defense regulations, security protocols, National Stock Numbers (NSNs), and how to precisely fill the needs dictated by the DoD regulations.

The GSA, on the other hand, is pivotal in acquiring goods to keep the government functioning as efficiently as possible (please don't chuckle too hard at that statement). Businesses engaging with the GSA must understand contracting vehicles like GSA Schedules, which provide a streamlined path for agencies to acquire a massive list of products and services frequently used by the GSA and the agencies it supports.

Beyond DoD and GSA, other agencies like HHS (Health & Human Services), DOT (Department of Transportation), and EPA (Environmental Protection Agency) focus on their own specific missions, opening an endless list of opportunities for businesses wanting to sell goods and services to the federal government. Recognizing each agency's requirements and regulations is vital for companies wishing to align their offerings with government needs.

DECENTRALIZED NATURE OF STATE AND LOCAL GOVERNMENTS

The government procurement arena extends to state and local governments across the country, each with unique processes and regulations that must be complied with when dealing with those specific entities. States, cities, and counties typically operate independently from one another, adding a new level of complexity to the arena.

While there will be similarities, each city, county, and state will have its own system for posting opportunities and its own method for a contractor to respond to those opportunities. While some have unique and exclusive online platforms that serve only their needs, others subscribe to larger privately operated platforms used by several governments and organizations. These larger platforms may serve several cities, counties, states, and other large organizations like colleges and universities.

The differences in acquisitions extend beyond processes and platforms, though. Different agencies may prioritize social initiatives over practical needs, community development projects over infrastructure requirements, or will focus primarily on local or regional economic development goals. Contractors must understand the agency's underlying goals and the strategic objectives for successful engagement.

Interactions with contracting officials and decision-makers within governments and large organizations differ from one to the next, but establishing effective communication channels and building relationships is essential for businesses navigating this decentralized landscape. Always remember that, ultimately, people do business with people. Often, it can be those relationships that make the difference between success and failure.

DIFFERENT TYPES OF GOVERNMENT CONTRACTS

Government contracts come in different types, each fulfilling the specific needs of the buying agency and determined by the nature of the products and services being purchased. This chapter briefly examines some kinds of contracts utilized in procurements of hard goods and products, including fixed-price agreements, blanket purchase agreements (BPAs), indefinite-delivery/indefinite-quantity (IDIQ) contracts, and some non-typical arrangements.

FIXED-PRICE AGREEMENTS

The most common type of contract found when selling
The most common type of contract found when selling products to government agencies is the fixed-price contract. Typically, fixed-price agreements will consist of two primary types of offerings: a set quantity of a specific item that requires a firm, fixed-price bid, or a predetermined budget amount wherein the buyer is looking for the highest number of the requested item that can be provided within that budget.

Fixed-price agreements offer stability and predictability by establishing a predetermined price for the items that are being purchased. The appeal for the buyer lies in budget predictability and the ease with which the purchase documents, fulfillment needs, and payment arrangements can be met by both the buying agent and the contractor providing the products.

Understanding fixed-price agreements requires a grasp of basic profit margin calculations and an ability to calculate costs and expenses accurately to avoid submitting bids that ultimately cause the contractors to lose money on the contracts. Success with Fixed-Price Agreements lies in a contractor's ability to effectively execute skillful project management and cost control measures.

SELL PRICE CALCULATOR FOR PRODUCTS

| | | | | | | | PROFIT MARGIN SELL PRICES PER ITEM | | | |
| | | ITEM | TOTAL | SHIPPING | MISCELLANEOUS | | 15% | 20% | 25% | 30% |
ITEM	QTY	COST	SHIPPING	PER ITEM	OTHER COSTS	TOTAL COST	MARGIN	MARGIN	MARGIN	MARGIN
Toilet Paper	20,000	$0.17	$752.52	$0.04	$0.00	$0.21	$0.24	$0.26	$0.28	$0.30

BPAs

Another standard vehicle for government contracting is the Blanket Purchase Agreement (BPA). BPAs serve as a mechanism to streamline and expedite government agencies' purchasing of goods and services. These pre-negotiated frameworks eliminate the necessity for repetitive negotiations or bidding by providing a structured and efficient approach for government agencies and contractors. Although the initial bidding and proposal submission methods are the same, the contracts are typically for a set assortment of products over an extended period. For example, a BPA for office supplies such as pens, paper, and staplers would establish a set price for each item and allow the agency to purchase those items when needed over a contracted period, such as one year. Normally, a BPA will also allow for optional extension time frames to avoid the bidding/proposal process when the initial contract expires. Extension option years will enable the contractor to establish price increases for inflation at the renewal time each year, and the options can extend as far out as 5 years.

For contractors, securing a BPA is more than just a contractual arrangement – it represents a gateway to a predictable and stable revenue stream over a specified period. The agreement creates a foundation for a long-term relationship with the government agency, offering a consistent business flow without continuous bidding on individual contracts.

When awarded a Blanket Purchase Agreement (BPA) in a government contract, contractors can enjoy several benefits that contribute to the efficiency and stability of their business operations. Here are some key advantages:

1. Streamlined procurement process: BPAs establish the exact items, specifications for those products, and the exact pricing by creating a pre-negotiated schedule for a contract. This allows the buying agency to order the specified products as needed without posting new bidding opportunities and going through the same compliance reviews every time that product is required.

2. Predictable revenue stream for contractors: Because these BPAs are long-term arrangements with preset pricing and cost factors, contractors can more effectively plan and allocate resources during the contract period, contributing to more financial stability.

3. Cost savings: With a BPA, contractors can achieve cost savings by purchasing larger inventory quantities, allowing for lower per-unit pricing on those items. Contractors also realize cost savings by focusing on fulfillment only, not being forced to procure, receive, stock,

and then fulfill to the buying agency for each subsequent order.

4. Formation of a strategic partnership: A BPA is more than just a contract for goods and commodities. It also represents a partnership between the buying agency and the awarded contractor that often leads to additional purchases outside the initial BPA's scope and even addendums to the existing agreement that were not included in the original RFP. Handled professionally, a contractor stands to earn far more business than what is specified at the beginning of the relationship.

In summary, being awarded a BPA contract provides contractors with a stable revenue stream, reduced bidding overhead, streamlined procurement processes, and the opportunity to establish a strategic and enduring partnership with the government agency. These benefits contribute to the overall success and sustainability of the contractor's engagements in the government procurement arena. They can be considered the ultimate prize in government contracts.

IDIQ CONTRACTS

Indefinite Delivery/Indefinite Quantity (IDIQ) contracts are another type of government contract highly valued and sought after by most contractors. These contracts are more complex in the bidding process and are often priced based on a set discount off of published prices. There is typically no set quantity or delivery schedule due to the nature of the products included in the offering. Some examples would be consumable office supplies, plastic flatware for dining facilities, and other consumable goods with hard-to-predict inventory flows.

Like BPAs, IDIQs offer contractors a more stable revenue stream over time. Still, because of the "Indefinite" characteristics of these contracts, the consistency of sales is more challenging to predict.

RFPs for IDIQ contracts require more attention to the details of the specific terms and conditions and a better understanding of the buying agency's ultimate goals and needs of the contract. Extensive planning involving the potential product needs by the contractor is essential for the long-term success of this type of project.

Contractors who excel in inventory and project management are exceptionally well suited to these agreements and should pursue them aggressively. It is also essential for a contractor to have well-established sources for all of the products included in the IDIQ contract to avoid supply issues later in the contract term.

Here are some examples of products that are commonly purchased by government agencies through IDIQ contracts:

1. Office Supplies

2. IT Equipment

3. Safety and Security equipment

4. Medical Supplies

5. Construction Materials

6. Maintenance and Repair Supplies

7. Scientific and Laboratory equipment

8. Training materials

9. Uniforms and apparel

These examples show a tiny sampling of the various products purchased with IDIQ contracts. The flexibility of these contracts allows the buying agencies the freedom to order as needed and not have to inventory mass quantities of supplies on-site.

In essence, IDIQ contracts establish a relationship between government agencies and contractors, offering a flexible and efficient means for addressing the changing needs of a specific organization. By understanding and harnessing the potential of IDIQ contracts, businesses can position themselves as responsive partners in fulfilling government agencies' diverse and evolving needs.

NON-TYPICAL ARRANGEMENTS

Although not very common in the contracting world, there are some non-typical contract types that businesses should become familiar with. Learning the basics about these types of contracts and their unique terminology will help expand the contractor's overall knowledge base and increase the ability to participate in larger, more advanced procurement projects.

Breaking from the traditional and more common landscape of fixed-price, BPA, and IDIQ contracts, unconventional models such as Public/Private Partnerships (PPPs) and Performance-Based Contracting introduce the contractor to a more complex and even creative method of government procurement. PPPs create collaborative efforts that typically address public service issues or infrastructure development, while Performance-Based Contracting shifts the focus to achieving specific outcomes for a government program with defined goals.

Diving into this unconventional side of government contracting can be an exciting and rewarding experience, but it requires a strong knowledge of the workings of the agencies pursued and an ability to create solutions to problems that these agencies might not have identified yet. Combining this inherent need for creative problem-solving with the complexities of government procurement regulations and compliance issues presents very unique challenges in the world of government contracting.

SPOTLIGHT ON THE FEDERAL ACQUISITION REGULATION (FAR)

An understanding of the Federal Acquisition Regulation (FAR) is essential to government contracting. Simply put, the FAR is a comprehensive and detailed set of rules and regulations governing federal government purchasing. This chapter will not be an exhaustive explanation or examination of the FAR but instead an introduction and an emphasis on how vital the FAR's role is in government contracting. Discussing specific regulations and explaining how they apply in government procurement would require thousands of pages and become the world's most excellent cure for insomnia.

A solid understanding of how the FAR applies to selling goods and commodities is essential for businesses venturing into government contracting. The FAR is the final word, the end-all, the absolute set-in-stone rules that must be complied with at all times.

The FAR encompasses various topics, from forming contracts to ethical considerations, compliance issues, and contract fulfillment and administration. As the FAR applies to selling tangible products to the government, contractors need to dive deep into the specific regulations highlighted on each RFP examined. These RFPs typically list any FARs expressly waived or amended for that particular RFP. While avoiding them completely or quickly scanning the FAR section lightly is easy to do, a contractor must be diligent and disciplined in focusing on the FAR sections of all RFPs they pursue.

There are several good resources available to a contractor when researching FARs. First and most important is the actual regulation itself. These can be found online at https://www.acquisition.gov and are organized in an easy-to-search fashion on the site. Beyond that site, simply executing an internet search for the needed regulation will reveal many articles, analyses, and explanations for just about any regulation.

One of the more common regulations that a contractor will have to deal with when selling products to the government is **DFARS 252.225-7036 Buy American—Free Trade Agreements—Balance of Payments Program.** Simply put, this regulation stipulates what countries of origin are acceptable for the products provided. Whether it mandates the products be made in the USA or allows products from a qualifying Trade Agreement Act country depends on the type of product, the size of the project in dollar amount, and which agency is purchasing the items. A current list of TAA-qualifying countries can be found in Appendix A at the end of this book or online at https://gsa.federalschedules.com/resources/taa-designated-countries

While there are regulations that are commonly used on almost all RFPs, it is crucial that a contractor read every paragraph carefully to make sure there aren't any unusual requirements on a particular project that must be complied with.

CHAPTER HIGHLIGHTS

1. Understand the roles and missions of different federal agencies and how those missions affect a contractor's approach to bidding on those RFPs.

2. Understand the differences between city, county, and state procurement vs. federal procurement opportunities.

3. Understand the basics of the different types of government contracts.

4. Understand the significance of building symbiotic relationships with government buyers and the importance of effective communication with those buyers.

5. Basic familiarity with the Federal Acquisition Regulation (FAR) and the importance of ensuring compliance with the FAR.

ACTION STEPS

1. Email or call the contracting officer on any or all of the RFPs you are currently working on and introduce yourself.
2. Pick one new (relevant) FAR daily for a week and spend 20-30 minutes reading and studying that FAR.
3. Search for and lightly peruse at least one opportunity for each contract type (Fixed-Price, BPA, and IDIQ) to help establish familiarity with how they are presented.

CHAPTER 2

FEDERAL REGISTRATION AND QUALIFICATIONS

Before businesses can bid on government contracts, they must complete the necessary registration processes. This chapter explores the significance of business registration and the steps involved in becoming a qualified government contractor.

SAM (SYSTEM FOR AWARD MANAGEMENT) REGISTRATION

As a business looking to pursue the avenue of government contracting, registering on the appropriate government sites and obtaining the necessary identification numbers are the first priorities. In addition to these registrations, acquiring specific set-aside certifications such as 8(a), Woman Owned, Service Disabled Veteran Owned, and various others will be invaluable to achieving success in the government procurement arena.

SAM stands for the System for Award Management. It is the primary gateway for businesses to get into the world of government contracts. SAM.gov is a giant online platform where the government checks out businesses before they can start bidding on contracts. It is also the largest single platform for opportunities companies can utilize to bid on government contracts. SAM.gov is like a one-stop shop that brings together government buyers and sellers in an easy-to-navigate format that makes government procurement much more accessible than ever before.

Getting registered on SAM.gov is the first big step into government contracting. Businesses wanting to pursue this market will create an account on SAM by giving some basic (but detailed) information about the business and by completing the registration process to obtain a UEI (Unique Entity Identifier) code. Once the UEI is secured, SAM.gov will take the company through the next step in obtaining a CAGE (Commercial and Government Entity Code) Code.

This CAGE code is also a prerequisite for bidding on any government contract.

In addition to securing both the UEI and the CAGE code, a business must renew both of them annually. There is no cost, but it is a step in the process that should be scheduled in advance with automatic reminders turned on to avoid any lapse in service.

The steps to register on SAM.gov are detailed below to make the process as easy as possible. While these steps are accurate at the time of this book's publication, be aware that some changes may occur over time, and be prepared if they differ slightly when registration is attempted.

Here's a step-by-step summary:

1. Access SAM.gov: Visit the official System for Award Management (SAM) website at (https://www.sam.gov/).

2. Create a User Account: If you don't have an existing SAM account, click on the "Create a User Account" option. Provide the necessary information to create your user account, including a valid email address.

3. Verify Email: Check your email for a verification message from SAM.gov. Follow the instructions in the email to verify your email address.

4. Login to SAM: Log in to SAM.gov using the credentials you created during the account setup.

5. Start Registration: Once logged in, navigate to the "Register/Update Entity" section. Click on the "Start Registration" button.

6. Determine Entity Type: Choose the appropriate entity type for your business, such as "Legal Business Name," "Government Entity," or "Individual."

7. Provide Basic Information: Enter basic information about your business, including its legal name, physical address, and other relevant details.

8. D-U-N-S Number: Input your Data Universal Numbering System (D-U-N-S) number. If your business doesn't have one, you may need to request it from Dun & Bradstreet (D&B) before proceeding.

9. Complete Core Data: Fill out the core data details, which include information about your business's size, ownership, and capabilities.

10. Financial Information: Provide financial information, including your business's financial stability and relevant details.

11. NAICS Codes: Select the North American Industry Classification System (NAICS) codes that best represent the products or services your business offers.

12. Electronic Funds Transfer (EFT): Enter Electronic Funds Transfer (EFT) information for payments related to federal contracts.

13. Points of Contact: Identify and provide information for points of contact within your business, including the primary and additional points of contact.

14. Review and Submit: Review all entered information for accuracy and completeness. Once satisfied, submit your registration.

15. Obtain CAGE Code: After submission, you may be prompted to request a Commercial and Government Entity (CAGE) code. Follow the instructions to obtain your CAGE code.

16. Confirmation and Updates: Once submitted, you will receive confirmation of your registration. Keep your information up to date by regularly revisiting SAM.gov and updating your registration as needed.

17. SAM.gov Assistance: If you encounter issues or have questions during the registration process, utilize the help resources provided on SAM.gov or contact the SAM Help Desk for assistance.

Always refer to the specific instructions provided on the SAM website, as the registration process details may be subject to updates or changes.

CAGE Code (Commercial Government and Entity Code)

The Commercial and Government Entity Code (CAGE) is a unique identifier code assigned to businesses or organizations looking to do business with the federal government. The CAGE code can be considered a personalized digital fingerprint for a company that allows the government to track its interactions with that business. The CAGE code acts as your "membership card" into government contracting, allowing you access to thousands of opportunities to submit bids and earn government business. Without a CAGE code, you are blocked from participating in these opportunities, at least at the federal level. A CAGE code is a prerequisite to doing business with the federal government. It is not a step that can be skipped.

The CAGE code is a fundamental part of the government procurement system. These codes allow the government to maintain a transparent (semi-), organized, and efficient system that is standardized across all federal procurement platforms. That is, at least in concept, the intent. Whether that is also the reality is up for debate.

While getting a CAGE code for a business is not difficult, specific requirements must be met to ensure eligibility. First, the company must be registered in SAM.gov and possess a UEI (Unique Entity Identifier) before attempting to secure a CAGE code. At the time of this writing, a business must also have a DUNS number issued by Dun & Bradstreet before applying for a CAGE code. This requirement could (and probably will) change soon as DNB has lost its long-term contract with the federal government, so be sure to check this online before you get a DUNS number. It may not be necessary.

Another requirement is that the address used in SAM.gov and when applying for the CAGE code must match exactly. It must be a physical address; even a home address is acceptable, but do not try to get a CAGE code with a virtual address or a mailing center address, as it will likely not be approved and can cause delays in processing.

Once the CAGE code has been issued, it can be used for various government contracting activities. It uniquely identifies the business entity and is required when bidding on government contracts.

It's been stated already, but always refer to the specific instructions provided on the SAM website, as the process details may be subject to updates or changes.

CERTIFICATIONS

In the world of government contracting, many businesses are becoming more aware of the benefits of the certifications available to both small and large companies. There is a long list of specific certifications available. Still, the most common is the 8(a) business development program, the hub zone certification, the woman-owned small business and economically disadvantaged woman-owned small business certifications, and the service-disabled veteran-owned small business certification.

8(A) BUSINESS DEVELOPMENT PROGRAM

The 8(a) business development program is designed to aid economically and socially disadvantaged small business owners. The federal government regulates the criteria for determining who is disadvantaged under this program. Those criteria can be studied in the Code of Federal Regulations Title 13 part 124-8(a).

Generally, the 8(a) program includes members of socially disadvantaged groups such as black Americans, Asian Pacific Americans, Hispanic Americans, Native Americans, and subcontinent asian americans. Also, the economically disadvantaged standards require a net worth of less than $850,000, adjusted gross income for three years of $400,000 or less, and total assets of $6,500,000 or less. Companies interested in applying for this certification can test their eligibility and whether it is a good fit for them by going to the Small Business Administration's website at https://certify.sba.gov and following the 8(a) program prompts.

HUBZONE CERTIFICATION

The HUBZone certification program focuses on businesses whose offices are in historically underutilized business zones. These companies can gain an advantage in federal contracting by earning this certification. For fiscal year 2023, the Small Business Administration published a goal of awarding at least 3% of all federal contract dollars to historically underutilized businesses. According to a recent release from the Biden administration, new goals are in place to move that number to exceed 5% annually.

To obtain HUBZone status, a business must be designated as a small business according to Small Business Administration standards, it must be at least 51% owned and controlled by U.S. citizens (or other eligible groups), and its principal office must be located in a hub zone. At least 35% of its employees must live in a hub zone.

Companies interested in applying for HUBZone certification can do so through the SBA website at https://www.sba.gov/federal-contracting/contracting-assistance-programs/hubzone-program

Businesses can also check the hub zone map on the same webpage to see if they are located in a qualifying area. This map was updated on July 1st, 2023, and some areas may have changed, so it is essential to check for updates before submitting an application.

WOMAN-OWNED SMALL BUSINESS CERTIFICATION

Another beneficial certification that can be obtained is the woman-owned small business certification offered by the federal government. This certification's intent is to help women or women-owned small businesses compete for federal contracts. This category also falls under the historically underutilized business label and is included in the targeted 5% of annual spending. To apply for this certification, a business must be registered in SAM.gov and then apply through the SBA website at WOSB.certify.sba.gov. The application will require certain documents to prove the business' eligibility, such as business structure, ownership and control, financial statements and tax returns, and proof of U.S. citizenship. A detailed checklist of the required documents can be found on the SBA website and companies should be prepared that this process can take up to 90 days to complete.

SERVICE DISABLED VETERAN OWNED SMALL BUSINESS

The eligibility requirements for this certification should be obvious. If the business is 51% owned and controlled by a service-disabled veteran, it could be eligible. Like the other certifications in the historically underutilized business categories, being certified as an SDVOSB can open many doors in the exclusive set-aside contracts and sole source contracts arena.

Like the other certifications previously mentioned, the eligibility requirements and application for the service-disabled veteran-owned small business program can be found on the Small Business Administration's website.

ADDING CERTIFICATIONS TO SAM.GOV PROFILE

The procedures and interfaces on government websites like SAM.gov may change, but based on the current procedures, here is the method used for adding certifications to a business profile in SAM.gov:

1. Log In to SAM.gov: Visit the SAM.gov website and log in using your credentials.

2. Access Your Entity Registration: Once logged in, navigate to your entity registration.

3. Navigate to the Certifications Section: Look for a section related to certifications or additional information.

4. Add Certifications: Click on the option to add or update certifications.

5. Provide Required Information: Follow the prompts to provide the necessary information. This may include details about the specific certification, certification number, issuing agency, and expiration date.

6. Upload Supporting Documents: Some certifications may require supporting documentation. Upload any required documents, ensuring they meet the specified format and size requirements.

7. Review and Confirm: Review the information you provided. Confirm that all details are accurate.

8. Submit the Changes: Once satisfied, submit the changes or updates to your SAM.gov profile.

9. Check for Confirmation: Look for a confirmation message or email indicating that your certifications have been successfully added or updated.

10. Regularly Update: Keep your certifications up to date by revisiting your SAM.gov profile regularly.

Remember that the exact steps may vary, and it's crucial to refer to the official SAM.gov guidance or contact SAM.gov support for the most precise instructions.

For the latest and most accurate information, visit the official SAM.gov website (https://www.sam.gov/).

CHAPTER HIGHLIGHTS

1. Completing registration on SAM.gov and securing a CAGE code are the essential first steps for a business venturing into government contracting.

2. SAM.gov Unique Entity Identifiers (UEI) and CAGE codes must be renewed annually.

3. Obtaining certain certifications can significantly enhance a company's prospects in government contracting.

ACTION STEPS

1. Register in SAM.gov and secure a CAGE code.

2. Research and pursue all relevant certifications that the business might be eligible for.

CHAPTER 3
REGISTRATION--CITY, COUNTY, AND STATE PLATFORMS

While the world of federal government contracting can be lucrative, businesses interested in selling their products to governments should also recognize cities, counties, and states as potential customers. In this chapter, we will explore the essential steps for finding city, county, and state procurement platforms and discuss how to register as bidders to begin the engagement with these smaller government agencies.

Most state and local governments manage their purchasing processes independently. This forces companies interested in doing business with them to search for and locate the specific platforms used. Most state and local organizations utilize digital systems, centralized websites, or dedicated portals to announce bidding opportunities, RFPs, and RFQs. Understanding the decentralized nature of state and local business adds labor to the initial process of registering as a vendor but also tends to make researching and bidding on opportunities easier than those at the federal level.

The easiest method for finding these platforms is to do an Internet search. Search terms such as "state of Texas procurement" or "doing business with the state of Texas" should produce search results that identify the exact websites to find these opportunities and place bids. There are several centralized websites that certain States and localities subscribe to that manage the procurement process outside of the state's official websites. The end of this chapter will list several procurement sites that serve multiple cities, states, colleges, and universities.

One downside to the decentralized nature of state and local contracting is that companies must register on many bidding websites based on how many different organizations they want to do business with. For example, the state of Texas does not use the same bidding site as the state of Louisiana, so to do business with both would require separate registrations on each site. The upside is that, typically, these registrations are speedy and straightforward to do. There is usually far less verification needed at this level of procurement.

CENTRALIZED PROCUREMENT PLATFORMS

While this list is not a complete list of procurement sites utilized nationwide, it is an excellent example of some that are very common and a great start for any business wanting to expand its access to state and local government bidding opportunities. It is highly recommended to use search engines to expand on this list and secure registrations on as many platforms as possible.

1. **BidNet Direct**: A centralized platform used by various state and local government agencies to post and manage procurement opportunities.
   Website: (https://www.bidnetdirect.com/)

2. **GovWin IQ:** Provides access to a database of government contracting opportunities, including those from state and local agencies.
   Website: (https://iq.govwin.com/)

3. **DemandStar:** Connects businesses with government agencies for procurement opportunities at the state and local levels.
   Website: (https://network.demandstar.com/)

4. **eMaryland Marketplace:** Maryland's procurement platform, offering opportunities from various state agencies.
   Website: (https://emaryland.buyspeed.com/bso/)

5. **Cal eProcure:** California's online marketplace for procurement, centralizing opportunities from state agencies.
   Website: (https://caleprocure.ca.gov/)

6. **Florida Vendor Bid System (FVBS):** Florida's centralized platform for vendors to access and respond to procurement opportunities.
   Website:
   (https://fvbs.po.myflorida.com/webapp/vssonline/AltSelfService)

7. **NYC Procurement Roadmap:** New York City's platform providing information on procurement opportunities and guidance for vendors.
Website: (https://vendornoir.cityofnewyork.us/frpp/)

8. **Pennsylvania's eMarketplace:** Centralized platform for vendors to register and access procurement opportunities in Pennsylvania.
Website: (https://www.emarketplace.state.pa.us/Solicitations.aspx)

9. **Texas SmartBuy:** Texas' centralized purchasing portal, offering a consolidated view of state procurement opportunities.
Website: (https://www.txsmartbuy.com/sp)

10. **Virginia eProcurement Portal:** Virginia's platform for electronic procurement, providing access to state agency solicitations.
Website: (https://eva.virginia.gov/)\

These platforms serve as valuable resources for businesses looking to engage with state and local government procurement opportunities across the United States. Companies must explore the platforms relevant to their target regions and industries.

CHAPTER HIGHLIGHTS

1. Most city, county, state, and university procurements are posted on exclusive buying platforms that are not listed on SAM.gov or other federal sites.
2. Thousands of bidding opportunities exist in the non-federal world of government contracting.

ACTION STEPS

1. Use internet search engines to locate city, county, and state procurement sites and register the business on each site.
2. Maintain a spreadsheet or log of each site the company registers in and include who the buying agency is (city, county, state, university name) and any user ID and password information.

CHAPTER 4

FEDERAL CONTRACT OPPORTUNITIES

This chapter should serve as a guide on how to locate, identify, and pursue bidding opportunities at the federal government levels. The federal contracting landscape offers several bidding platform options, such as SAM.gov, DIBBS (the Defense Information Bidding System), and GPO.gov, while the local and state landscape is even more widespread, with hundreds of bidding sites available and will be addressed in the next chapter. The skills learned to search and identify bidding opportunities within a company's areas of expertise should be universal across all platforms.

FEDERAL CONTRACTING PLATFORMS

Understanding the differences in the critical platforms for federal contract opportunities is essential. Sam.gov is the primary portal that consolidates various federal government procurement systems into one centralized platform. DIBBS, managed by the Defense Logistics Agency or DLA, serves as the central hub for defense-related solicitations gpo.gov is responsible for procuring goods and services within the realm of publications and printed merchandise. It is essential to note that these platforms and the landscapes that they entail evolve over time, and these platforms could change as the government sees fit. Staying informed about updates and complying with new registration requirements is imperative for a contractor to maintain relevance in the government contracting arena.

NAVIGATING SAM.GOV FOR CONTRACT BIDDING

Locating, researching, and bidding on contract opportunities through sam.gov is a process that requires careful consideration by companies pursuing these contracts. Simply opening sam.gov and scrolling through the thousands of opportunities is, at best, inefficient and, at worst, a complete nightmare that will discourage any business from pursuing government contracting further. It is essential that a company understands what types of contracts it is seeking and the associated NAICS codes assigned to those contracts when searching through contract opportunities on sam.gov and any other government procurement website.

Once a business identifies these specific areas it wants to pursue, searching for opportunities within them is relatively simple. The SAM.gov home page has a link titled "contract opportunities." The contract opportunities search page allows for several filters to be used when searching to drill down through the thousands of postings and locate only those opportunities that are relevant to the business that is searching. Using these filters may take practice to learn what works best. Still, it is the same as any other search feature most Internet users are familiar with.

One of the more valuable features a business can use when opportunities are located is the "follow" feature at the top of each opportunity. Clicking this will ensure any addendums, updates, or changes to the opportunity will be sent to the business via e-mail when they are made. A company can also download each opportunity individually for a more detailed examination.

All opportunities posted on sam.gov will list the notice ID number, which buying agency posted the notice, any set-asides that are assigned to the opportunity, and all relevant dates, such as the original posting date and the response due date. They will also list the appropriate NAICS codes and a description of the opportunity so a company can know immediately if it's an appropriate opportunity to pursue. At the bottom of the opportunities posted will be the primary and secondary points of contact for any questions a potential bidder may have.

All in all, the sam.gov website should be relatively simple for anyone with basic Internet and computer skills.

UTILIZING DIBBS FOR DEFENSE-RELATED CONTRACTS

The defense information bidding system (DIBBS) stands out as a pivotal resource for businesses looking to secure defense-related contracts. However, maximizing the potential of DIBBS requires in-depth knowledge and intense self-education to become comfortable navigating the complexities of that system. DIBBS is considered by many to be one of the most complex and complicated platforms on which to pursue government contracting opportunities, but with that complexity comes the benefits of larger contracts and potentially more significant profit margins. To maximize their potential, businesses aiming to secure defense-related contracts through DIBBS must focus on several key elements.

First, understanding how DIBBS operates, including its functionalities, categories, and the entire procurement process, is essential. There is no shortcut method for obtaining this understanding. The only absolute path is for a business to search for, locate, and read all aspects of DIBBS offerings to become proficient.

Second, conducting detailed market research on potential opportunities is also crucial. Locating a posting for a specific product may not be the best opportunity for a business if that product historically has hundreds of bidders and tiny profit margins on previous contracts. Delving deep into the historical data can guide a company in selecting the best opportunities for them.

Finally, compliance and regulatory issues will differ when bidding on defense-related contracts. Companies that don't research these issues in detail are potentially bidding with significant risk to their existence. It is essential to have a complete and comprehensive understanding of any applicable regulations to maintain compliance and avoid severe legal issues moving forward.

By approaching DIBBS opportunities with a well-informed and strategic mindset, businesses can position themselves to effectively compete for and secure defense-related contracts. It requires focus, discipline, and a patient approach to becoming well-educated.

NATIONAL STOCK NUMBER SYSTEM (NSN)

The national stock number (NSN) system is a critical component of the Defense Information Bidding System (DIBBS), providing a standardized method for identifying and cataloging products purchased by the Department of Defense. Using the National Stock Number system in DIBBS is crucial for companies seeking to participate in defense-related purchases of goods and commodities.

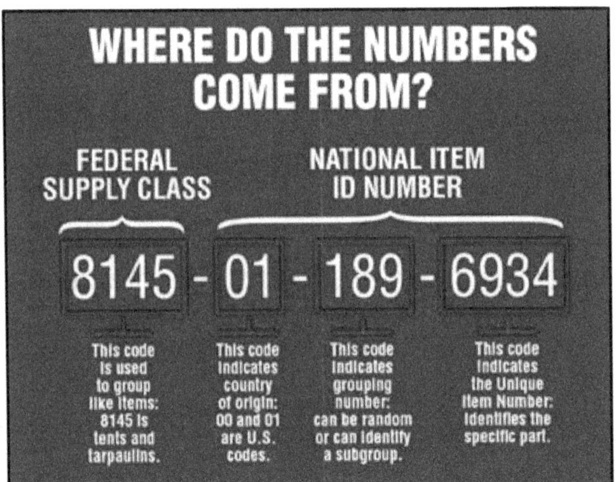

The NSN is a unique 13-digit numeric code that identifies explicitly each item of supply purchased and used by the US government. It includes information about the item's classification, part number, and country of origin.

Businesses can access NSN detailed information within DIBBS to identify specific items, research associated solicitations, review previous contract information, and understand any unique procurement requirements. Within the DIBBS platform, users can search for bidding opportunities based on specific NSN codes. By using these particular codes, businesses can focus their search efforts on products they are familiar with and may have easy access to.

By leveraging a comprehensive understanding of how the NSN system works and what products within the system are relevant to a company's offerings, navigating the defense procurement landscape becomes more efficient and potentially more profitable.

DISCOVERING OPPORTUNITIES THROUGH GPO.GOV

For businesses immersed in printing, publishing, and related services or accessing those services through trusted subcontractors, the US government publishing office gpo.gov is an effective gateway into government contracting.

In the field of printing and publishing, gpo.gov offers five different types of opportunities that companies can bid on:

1. **One-time bids:** One-time bids represent more considerable standalone and complex

procurement opportunities and are typically opportunities that require a much more formal and comprehensive RFP response.

2. **Term Contracts:** Term contracts support repetitive orders for a similar product or service over a pre-determined period. These can be from one to five years, and they each allow four simple, convenient orders directly from the buying agency to the contractor once that contract is established. Contract prices are fixed for the contract. And are typically adjusted for inflation within the original formal response. RFP responses for term contracts generally are more detailed and comprehensive than a standard RFQ.

3. **Simplified Purchase Agreements (SPA):** Simplified Purchase Agreements allow vendors to sign up on a list so that buying agents can purchase directly from those vendors without going through the formal bid posting process. Vendors wanting to be on this list must go through an application and approval process.

4. **GPO Onsite and Consulting Services:** This program is an umbrella agreement giving qualified GPO vendors a chance to provide onsite document solutions and consulting to federal government agencies. These contracts often include putting vendors in a position to offer comprehensive strategies for streamlining document operations within the federal government.

5. **Small Purchases:** The Small Purchases, or Quick Quote program, is by far the most prolific and most accessible program in which to participate on gpo.gov. Most GPO purchases under $100,000 are posted through this program. Quick Quote allows vendors to bid on many different opportunities daily. The bidding platform is straightforward and requires only a price for the requested items.

Gpo.gov offers a range of contracting opportunities for companies of all sizes and specialties. These programs can be quickly accessed when searching for opportunities that fit a contractor's offerings.

CHAPTER 5
CITY, COUNTY, AND STATE OPPORTUNITIES

When people think of government contracting, they often imagine the grandeur and complexity of federal contracts, with their massive projects and intricate systems like SAM.gov and DIBBS, alongside the high-stakes bidding processes. However, beyond the federal level, there lies a hidden treasure trove of business prospects at the state and local levels waiting to be explored. These opportunities stem from an array of state governments, counties, cities, and other local entities that together create a vibrant ecosystem ripe for business.

Consider the sheer numbers: the United States is home to 50 states, 14 territories, 3,143 counties, 421 metropolitan statistical areas, and approximately 2,500 cities with populations exceeding 10,000, amounting to over 6,000 distinct government organizations. Each of these entities requires a wide range of goods and services to function effectively, from everyday essentials like office supplies, technology gadgets, and janitorial products to consumables such as toilet paper and soap. These needs present a vast array of opportunities for businesses to make an impact, supporting local schools, libraries, public works departments, and more.

State and local contracts offer several advantages, including the sheer volume of opportunities, with thousands of potential doors opening for business in every state, county, and city. These contracts often come with the benefit of ease of fulfillment, as they tend to be more straightforward than their federal counterparts, featuring less daunting paperwork and faster processes. Additionally, the competition at this level is usually less fierce, allowing smaller businesses to find their niche and thrive. Securing a local contract means directly contributing to the well-being of your community, tapping into diverse markets with unique needs, and building personal relationships that go beyond being just another bidder. Each locality has its own unique requirements, whether it's road maintenance equipment, school furniture, or software licenses, providing a market waiting to be served.

The opportunities within state and local government contracts represent not merely transactions but partnerships. They offer a significant avenue for both budding entrepreneurs and established businesses to explore and potentially unlock the key to their next successful venture.

DECENTRALIZED PLATFORMS

Diving into the realm of state and local government contracting opens up a world of opportunities for businesses looking to expand their horizons beyond the federal level. However, navigating this landscape requires an understanding of its unique characteristics, especially its decentralized nature, which stands in stark contrast to the more centralized procurement processes of the federal government.

At the federal level, businesses are accustomed to a uniform system where centralized platforms, such as SAM.gov, serve as one-stop shops for finding and bidding on contracts. These platforms streamline the process, making it relatively straightforward for businesses to identify opportunities, submit bids, and manage contracts under a common set of procedures.

In contrast, the state and local levels operate through a wide variety of procurement platforms, reflecting the diverse and decentralized nature of these government entities. Each state, county, and city may have its own approach to procurement, with some developing their own platforms and others opting to use standardized platforms managed by private companies. This diversity means that businesses looking to tap into these markets must first undertake the task of identifying which platforms are used by their target governments.

For businesses venturing into these waters, maintaining a detailed record of the platforms each government entity uses is crucial. This not only helps in keeping track of where to find potential opportunities but also aids in managing the login information required for each platform. Given the high number of platforms, it's common for businesses to end up with a collection of separate login credentials. To avoid confusion and ensure smooth access to these platforms, keeping a backup record of all login details is advisable. This practice can be a lifesaver, preventing potential disruptions in accessing the platforms and, by extension, bidding on new contracts.

The process of registering as a vendor or supplier on these various platforms can vary significantly. Some platforms make the registration process a breeze, requiring only basic company information such as the name, address, Employer Identification Number (EIN), contact number, etc. Once this information is submitted, businesses can often immediately begin exploring and bidding on contracts. However, other platforms might necessitate additional steps, including the submission of verification documents or undergoing a review and approval process by the platform's administrators. These extra requirements, while potentially adding to the workload, are designed to ensure the integrity and competitiveness of the bidding process.

Despite the challenges posed by the need to manage multiple login credentials and navigate through different registration processes, the effort can be well worth it. The state and local government contracting arena is rich with opportunities for businesses of all sizes. By understanding and adapting to the decentralized nature of these procurement processes, businesses can unlock a plethora of opportunities to grow and succeed.

Toward the end of this chapter, a list is provided of several popular procurement platforms that cater to state and local government contracts. This list will serve as a starting point for businesses looking to explore the diverse opportunities available at the state and local levels.

STATE AND LOCAL REGULATIONS AND GUIDELINES

Navigating the landscape of state and local government contracting also means grappling with the diverse array of buying processes and regulations that each entity employs. This variety introduces additional layers of complexity for businesses aiming to sell their products or services to these governments. It's crucial for companies to thoroughly understand and adhere to the specific rules and regulations of each buying organization they wish to engage with. Failing to comply can lead to a range of consequences, from being disqualified from a bid for minor infractions to facing significant financial penalties for more serious violations. Therefore, maintaining compliance is not just a matter of legal obligation but a key factor in ensuring the long-term success of a contractor in the government procurement arena.

Most smaller government entities that extend procurement opportunities tend to accept responses to Requests for Proposals (RFPs) and Requests for Quotations (RFQs) digitally via their online platforms. This digital submission process, while convenient, requires bidders to be meticulous in understanding and following the submission guidelines laid out by the buying organization.

Responding to an RFQ typically involves providing a price quote for the requested items along with a succinct description to enable the buyer to ascertain whether the offerings meet the specifications set forth in the RFQ. The process is designed to be straightforward, provided that the vendor pays close attention to the requirements.

On the other hand, RFP responses usually demand a more comprehensive package of information. This might include documents such as Capability Statements, references, detailed technical descriptions of the products or services offered, and extensive pricing breakdowns. These documents can often be uploaded directly through the procurement platform or, in some cases, emailed to the contracting officer overseeing the RFP. The key to a successful RFP submission lies in the bidder's ability to carefully review and comply with all the instructions and requirements detailed in the RFP document. Overlooking or disregarding any part of these instructions can result in disqualification for non-compliance.

In summary, while the digital bidding process for state and local government contracts offers a streamlined avenue for submitting proposals, it demands a high level of attention to detail from contractors. Understanding and adhering to each buying organization's unique set of rules and regulations is essential for avoiding pitfalls and building a successful track record in government contracting.

BUILDING RELATIONSHIPS

Cultivating solid relationships is usually easier and often pays more dividends in the future when working with governments at the state level and below. These governments have more flexibility when purchasing and are not always required to post every need to a bidding platform. While each entity will have different guidelines, it is common for purchases below a certain threshold amount to be executed without a formal bidding process and instead done directly with vendors who have shown a history of providing value to the organization and have established a strong working relationship with the individuals within that agency. In these instances, the buyer often executes a sole-source purchase order to that preferred vendor. This saves the buying agency time, labor, and processing costs and affords the vendor new business without the added effort of producing a response to an RFP or an RFQ.

Specific Platforms

Some city and state procurement sites are listed below:

1. BidNet Direct: A centralized platform used by various state and local government agencies to post and manage procurement opportunities.

Website: (https://www.bidnetdirect.com/)

2. GovWin IQ: Provides access to a database of government contracting opportunities, including those from state and local agencies.

Website: (https://iq.govwin.com/)

3. DemandStar: Connects businesses with government agencies for procurement opportunities at the state and local levels.

Website: (https://network.demandstar.com/)

4. eMaryland Marketplace: Maryland's procurement platform, offering opportunities from various state agencies.

Website: (https://emaryland.buyspeed.com/bso/)

5. Cal eProcure: California's online marketplace for procurement, centralizing opportunities from state agencies.

Website: (https://caleprocure.ca.gov/)

6. Florida Vendor Bid System (FVBS): Florida's centralized platform for vendors to access and respond to procurement opportunities.

Website: (https://fvbs.po.myflorida.com/webapp/vssonline/AltSelfService)

7. NYC Procurement Roadmap: New York City's platform provides information on procurement opportunities and guidance for vendors.

Website: (https://vendornoir.cityofnewyork.us/frpp/)

8. Pennsylvania's eMarketplace: Centralized platform for vendors to register and access procurement opportunities in Pennsylvania.

Website: (https://www.emarketplace.state.pa.us/Solicitations.aspx)

9. Texas SmartBuy: Texas' centralized purchasing portal, offering a consolidated view of state procurement opportunities.

Website: (https://www.txsmartbuy.com/sp)

10. Virginia eProcurement Portal: Virginia's platform for electronic procurement, providing access to state agency solicitations.

Website: (https://eva.virginia.gov/)

A complete list of U.S. state procurement sites is available at:

The Institute for Public Procurement:

https://www.nigp.org/our-profession/state-and-provinces-procurement-websites

These platforms serve as crucial gateways for vendors to explore and bid on city and state contracts, providing valuable opportunities to engage with government agencies and secure contracts in various regions.

CHAPTER HIGHLIGHTS

1. Most city, county, state, and university procurements are posted on exclusive buying platforms that are not listed on SAM.gov or other federal sites.

2. Thousands of bidding opportunities exist in the non-federal world of government contracting.

ACTION STEPS

1. Use internet search engines to locate city, county, and state procurement sites and register the business on each site.

2. Maintain a spreadsheet or log of each site the company registers in and include who the buying agency is (city, county, state, university name) and any user ID and password information.

CHAPTER 6

GOVERNMENT PROCUREMENT METHODS

Developing a complete understanding of government contracting is necessary to have at least a general familiarity with the different methods of procurement the government uses. This chapter touches on several of those methods and details the most common. As complex as it may appear at first glance, each method serves a specific purpose and is very straightforward in execution. Studying the following sections should provide enough general knowledge on these methods so that a contractor can feel comfortable moving forward on each type's opportunities.

COMPETITIVE BIDDING

Most government purchasing is done through a competitive bidding process. From RFPs requiring detailed and complex technical responses to very simple RFQs requiring only a price bid, competitive bidding is the standard method for awarding contracts to businesses participating in the bidding process. Contract bidding can be much more than a simple "lowest bidder" situation. Reviewing the Evaluation Criteria on every opportunity examined is essential to build an understanding of how awards are determined. Some are decided by the "Lowest price technically acceptable" (LPTA), which awards the contract to the lowest bidder whose offering meets all requested specifications. Other factors may be evaluated, but the offers are not ranked based on non-cost/price factors. Different evaluation criteria provide bidders with a scoring system that could consider factors such as performance history, history with this specific buying agency, turnaround time of production and shipping, responses from references provided, and many other aspects that could be judged by the contracting officer and the buying agency. Understanding a specific RFP's evaluation criteria is crucial before preparing a response.

Competitive bidding processes vary greatly throughout government contracting, but most are now done digitally. Some agencies still want a physical sealed bid package sent in, but they are becoming rarer as technology advances. However, It is common for a buyer to request a sample of the items being proposed before the bid closing date. In those situations, the bidder must mail a product sample for consideration in the bidding award process.

Digital bidding can be a simple price entry on one website page or uploading a completed RFP response packet with multiple separate documents included. Whichever is needed, modern computer technology has made the bidding process far more accessible than in the past. This is another area in which a bidder must read and understand the bidding process detailed in an RFP so that compliance is not an issue. It is common for an entire bid packet to be disqualified simply for not following the submission guidelines listed in the offering.

SOLE-SOURCE CONTRACTS

Suppose a buying agent determines that only one supplier is available or capable of meeting the government's requirements on a specific contract. In that case, a Sole Source contract can be awarded. By law, when awarding a Sole Source contract, the contracting officer must provide a written justification explaining why the contract is being awarded outside of the competitive bidding process.

Sole source contracts are typically reserved for larger contracts such as military hardware or advanced computer software packages. Still, there are instances in which a more minor purchase could be deemed eligible for a sole source award. One example would be if only one manufacturer produces a specific item that the government needs, and they are the only source to obtain that item. Another would be in the case of a mandatory Set Aside, such as Woman Owned Small Business or Service Disabled Veteran Owned Business, and through the bidding process, it is determined that only one qualifying bidder is available. Sole source contracts, while challenging to secure initially, are highly sought after in government contracting.

INDEFINITE DELIVERY/INDEFINITE QUANTITY (IDIQ) CONTRACT

Government contracts that require on-call (or as-needed) services or consumable products with an unknown total quantity or turn rate are often awarded as Indefinite Delivery/Indefinite Quantity (IDIQ) contracts. IDIQ contracts are typically open-ended regarding how often or frequently a product or service is required. Still, the IDIQ will have a definite fixed period for which orders can be executed under the agreement. When a contractor is awarded an IDIQ, subsequent orders under that contract are accomplished by issuing a Delivery Order for product-based contracts or a Task Order for service-based contracts.

Some examples of IDIQ contracts include office supplies, disposable paper items, and consumables with no set depletion rate. Service-based IDIQs can consist of architecture services, maintenance contracts, and staffing agreements, for example. Government agencies issue IDIQ contracts when they need help determining how much or how much of a desired product or service they will require throughout the contract. Despite the unknown quantities, the contract will typically mandate a set minimum and maximum amount to be purchased. IDIQ contracts are issued for a predetermined number of "base" years with renewal options for additional years. Still, these types of contracts usually are at most a total of five years in duration.

MULTIPLE AWARD CONTRACTS (MACs)

Another common type of government contracting, specifically at the federal level, is the Multiple Award Task Order Contract, or MATOC. A MATOC is simply a contract with multiple awardees and is a particular type of IDIQ (Indefinite Delivery Indefinite Quantity) contract. Under a

MATOC, multiple awardees are chosen to provide specific products (or groups of products) or services within a predefined dollar amount set when the award is given.

Under a MATOC, multiple awardees are chosen using a standard proposal submission process to provide goods or services within a predefined dollar amount. Awardees consist of a pool of contractors who have won a spot on the team and will be given subsequent task orders or delivery orders that fall within the Scope of Work detailed in the RFP. Awarded contractors for MATOC service contracts will receive Task Orders, while contractors for products-oriented contracts will receive Delivery Orders. MATOCs are often chosen by the buying agency because they provide an additional layer of competition for the task order or delivery order awards that will be issued under the contract. MATOCs are often used by the military for purchasing construction supplies, maintenance services, and services and supplies related to facility design projects.

An essential aspect of MATOCs is that a contractor must secure its place on the list of awarded vendors before it can compete for the subsequent Task Orders or Delivery Orders. Most MATOCs have a five to ten-year performance period, so it's critical for a company to identify must-win contracts early in the process to allow sufficient time and resources to create a competitive response to the agency's initial RFP. Meeting with the buying agency before submitting a response, whether in person or through a phone conference, can be crucial in understanding their goals with the contract, the potential acquisition strategy, and any issues or hot buttons they may have for this project.

Once the MATOC solicitation is released, a company should submit its response just as it would on any other extensive RFP, focusing on the known issues and critical points discovered during the meeting with the buyers. Securing a MATOC can provide long-term stability and revenue for a business willing to devote the necessary time and resources to an effective response.

BLANKET PURCHASE AGREEMENTS (BPAS)

Blanket Purchase Agreements (BPAs) are a common type of government contract utilized to purchase open market services and supplies for which there is an anticipated repetitive need and the purchase falls below the simplified acquisition threshold (SAT). For 2024, the SAT has been increased to $250,000. (Recent averages in government spending show that simplified acquisitions exceed $460,000,000 annually.) BPAs establish "charge accounts" with awarded vendors for items or services included in the Statement of Work.

The underlying purpose of BPA is to reduce administrative costs for repetitive small purchases by eliminating the need to post a separate RFP and issue a new contract for each purchase. When the government agency knows in advance that they will be using the same service or products over and over, it is much simpler and more efficient for the agency to issue a BPA than to write a new contract each time.

BPAs are excellent options for both government agencies and vendors/contractors. By eliminating the need to prepare solicitations, search for sources, and create a synopsis for every acquisition, agencies can save significant amounts of time and money by utilizing BPAs. Awarded contractors can similarly save time and money by stocking inventory, utilizing volume cost savings with their supply chain, and establishing efficient order processes with a predictable revenue stream over a set period. Benefits of BPAs include:

- Provide opportunities to negotiate improved discounts
- Satisfy recurring requirements
- Reduce administrative costs by eliminating repetitive acquisition efforts
- Permit ordering activities to leverage buying power through volume purchasing
- Enable ordering activities by streamlined ordering procedures
- Reduce procurement lead time

COOPERATIVE PURCHASING AGREEMENTS

The federal Cooperative Purchasing Program allows eligible government agencies to use available budgeted funds to purchase needed products and services from pre-approved industry sources across jurisdictions. This program enables local, tribal, and state agencies, public educational institutions, and a select few other government agents to purchase products for specific categories, including security, law enforcement, and IT, through pre-negotiated cooperative purchasing agreements. This type of procurement can benefit government buyers by realizing lower administrative costs in both time and money, more favorable terms and conditions with the selected suppliers, and overall reduced price of purchased products. Contractors on the cooperative vendor lists can also benefit significantly from increased volume and lower production costs attributed to the ability to scale up for those larger quantities delivered over time through the agreement.

Most cooperative purchases exist in one of two primary forms: "Joint Solicitation" and "piggybacking." A Joint Solicitation occurs when two or more government buyers combine their anticipated product and service needs into a single offering. Each agency is then bound to the terms, conditions, and pricing included in the contract that emerges from this collaboration. Government buyers can realize significant savings by joining each other to increase the total quantities of items ordered through the contract.

"Piggybacking" occurs when an agency uses another agency's existing contract to execute a purchase for a service or product even though the buying agency was not included in the original solicitation and award. Agencies that piggyback on another contract are bound by the pricing, terms, and conditions set in the original agreement. While piggybacked orders are usually welcomed and appreciated by the contractor, they do not allow for forecasted sales and predictable revenue to the contractor and, therefore, rarely improve the pricing presented in the contract.

SMALL BUSINESS SET-ASIDES

In government contracting, small business set-asides play an essential role in the government's efforts to support small businesses. As long as at least two competitive companies can provide the products or services requested by a government agency, those contracts valued at less than $250,000 are automatically and exclusively set aside for small businesses, as defined by the Small Business Administration. Suppose there is only one company capable of providing for the contract. In that case, a Sole Source contract that still falls under the small business set-aside guidelines may be issued. The standards for being classified as a small business vary by industry. Still, they are determined by the number of employees and the annual revenues reported by the business.

Several programs and certifications exist that qualify for small business set-asides. These include the 8(a) program, Women-Owned Small Business, and Service Disabled Veteran Owned Small Business. Chapter 2 of this book, Federal Registration and Qualifications, details these certifications.

Contract value	Small business set-aside requirement
$10,00 to $250,000	Automatically and exclusively set aside for small businesses
$250,000 or more	Set aside if there are two or more small businesses that could do the work. (You must first consider 8(a), HUBZone, SDVO, and WOSB set-asides.)
$750,000 or more (non-construction contracts)	If not set aside for small business, must have a subcontracting plan if awarded to a non-small business
$1.5 million or more (construction contracts)	If not set aside for small business, must have a subcontracting plan if awarded to a non-small business

When assigning set-asides for an offering, there is no order of preference other than the stated goals for the agency assigning the set-aside. In 2024, the federal government has a government-wide goal of 23% of all contracts to be set aside for small businesses. That 23% goal includes specific group goals as follows:

Small Disadvantaged Businesses (8a Program)--at least 5%

Woman-Owned Small Businesses (WOSB)--at least 5%

Service-Disabled Veteran-Owned Businesses—at least 3%

Businesses in HUBZones (historically underutilized business zones)--at least 3%

Each agency tracks its penetrations into these categories and can adjust set-aside requirements to meet or exceed these goals.

Not all set-asides are for prime contracts (dealing directly with a government agency). Often, small businesses can find lucrative opportunities by subcontracting with a larger company awarded a prime contract. One example is an automotive manufacturer that has secured a sizeable prime contract to build Army jeeps but utilizes small business subcontractors to supply some parts. Small business set-aside opportunities are plentiful at all levels of government procurement. They are a valuable source of revenue for companies trying to break into government contracting.

Set-asides matter because they encourage a much more level playing field in government contracting and allow smaller companies to compete in an arena previously dominated by giant corporations. Set-asides also have been shown to foster economic growth and innovation in areas historically overlooked by government procurement.

GSA SCHEDULES

GSA Schedule contracts are indefinite delivery, indefinite quantity (IDIQ) contracts, meaning there is no limit on how much can be sold to the government or for how long. GSA Schedule contracts are a part of the General Service Administration's Multiple Award Schedule (MAS) program. The GSA Schedules program was created to establish long-term government-wide contracts with commercial firms, providing federal, state, and local government buyers access to more than 12 million products and services at discount pricing. The GSA Schedules program often allows for shorter lead times and improved transaction transparency, making the procurement process more efficient for government buyers and commercial contractors.

Since the GSA Schedules program makes it easy for government buyers to procure millions of solutions quickly at discounted prices, it is one of the most popular government contract vehicles. For FY2023, GSA contracts set a new spending record, with approximately $40 billion procured through the GSA Schedules program from over 12,000 commercial contractors.

GSA Schedule contractors range from Fortune 500 companies to small emerging domestic and international businesses. Once a company is awarded a GSA Schedule contract, it can have it for up to 20 years, making it a valuable long-term partnership between government agencies and commercial businesses.

A GSA Schedule contract enables a business to sell products or services to ANY agency of the federal government, specific other organizations, and state and local governments. Being awarded a GSA Schedule contract is long and laborious, often costing businesses large amounts of money and taking years to secure. The initial qualifications are that a company has operated for over two years and produces more than $150,000 in revenue annually. Beyond that, the process is long and detailed and requires a company to jump through many red tape hoops before even securing the contract. Pursuing a GSA Schedule is not for the faint of heart, but achieving this can translate to lucrative and long-term success for the winning company.

OTHER PROCUREMENT TYPES

In addition to the eight contract types listed in this chapter, other more seldomly used contract types exist that a contractor could experience and should at least be aware of. Federal Supply Schedules (FSSs) are another type of long-term contract similar to GSA Schedules. Government-Wide Acquisition Contracts (GWACs) are typically IT-related and accessible as a purchase vehicle to agencies across the federal procurement landscape. Finally, some government agencies have specialized procurement processes that a contractor should become aware of if bidding on a package for one of these departments. With many different contract types within government procurement, the only safe way for a business to navigate these is to read every offering line-by-line and examine every detail before committing to a response or bid. The responsibility falls solely on the bidding business, so ensuring a thorough understanding of the opportunity is essential to the business's long-term success.

CHAPTER HIGHLIGHTS

1. There is a wide variety of contract types within government contracting and successful contractors have, at minimum, a familiarization with each of those types.

2. Set asides make up at least 23% of all government contracts. Taking the steps necessary to secure one of the offered certifications is a valuable move for any business desiring growth in the government contracting space.

ACTION STEPS

1. Review all qualifications for securing one of the set-aside certifications and, if eligible, complete the steps necessary to secure one of those for the business.

2. Select several RFPs and review them in detail, focusing on any set-asides listed and what type of contract is being offered. This activity will help build more familiarity with the different contract types.

CHAPTER 7
UNDERSTANDING RFPs & RFQs

PURPOSE OF RFQs AND RFPs

RFPs (Request for Proposal) and RFQs (Request for Quote) serve as official invitations to businesses by government agencies when the agency needs to buy a product or service. These invitations are important because they tell companies exactly what the government wants and how they want it done, generally in a very detailed way. While there can be minor differences in how RFPs and RFQs are presented, they typically have similar goals and purposes.

First, the ultimate goal is to present an opportunity fairly, ensuring that all qualified businesses have the same chance to submit a bid on the contract being offered. The details of the request are laid out in such a way as to prevent special treatment or insider benefit from being given to one company over another. Not all businesses might be qualified or have access to the requested products or services. Still, they can decide if the offering is a good fit for them and if it's worth the effort required to submit a bid.

Secondly, these offerings are about getting the best deal for the taxpayers' money. By creating a competitive environment, the issuing government agency is creating a situation that guarantees the best overall value is secured, whether that value is price-driven or evaluated on a combination of price and quality factors.

Last, these documents publish all necessary regulations and guidelines for the offering to ensure that every bidder follows the same set of rules. This is where a thorough examination of the offering is crucial, as all are different regarding which regulations are required and which are not on each contract. Businesses must pay close attention to these regulations to avoid pitfalls further along in the process and maintain compliance when submitting offers and performing under the rules of the contracts awarded.

COMPONENTS OF RFQS AND RFPS

Understanding the critical components of RFPs and RFQs is essential for a business to respond effectively. Compliance with regulations is important, but compliance with the written instructions within the offering is just as vital to any chances for success in bidding on these contracts. While there is some variance in titles, order of presentation, and what may or may not be included in a government request, these documents typically incorporate some form of the following sections that must be understood and complied with in the final vendor's response:

1. Introduction: This section provides an overview of the procurement and the general needs of the purchasing agency. This will typically include the contract number, type,

and terms, along with any cover page that sets the context for the entire RFP. This can also contain the agency's mission, objectives, background information, and specific set-asides or qualification requirements for interested vendors. Also included should be opening and closing dates and any other pertinent timelines the bidding companies must know.

2. Scope of Work (SOW): The Scope of Work is the heart of the RFP and outlines the specific tasks or products, responsibilities, and deliverables required for a project. Often, the SOW will detail the exact problem or challenge the government agency is trying to address and the goals associated with that challenge. This section will list the technical specifications, specific performance standards required, and the exact deliverables expected of the provider upon contract award.

3. Evaluation Criteria: Every government contract opportunity will list the evaluation criteria used to judge proposals and how the contract will be awarded. A company needs to understand these criteria and tailor their offering to take advantage of how the bids will be judged. While cost is always listed as at least one of the aspects being considered, other factors such as technical expertise, past performance, disadvantaged business certifications held, the place or method of manufacturing, and many others can be just as important or even more important to the awarding agency. Understanding what the buying agency is looking for is necessary to build a competitive response to the RFP.

4. Terms and Conditions: This section will specify the legal and contractual requirements governing the procurement, including payment terms, any intellectual property rights, and warranties required for compliance.

5. Instructions to Vendors: Normally, an RFP will include precise instructions to vendors on submitting a response or bid and all the necessary information a business needs to produce an acceptable response. This section will often detail whether a response should be submitted online or in physical form, if and what samples may be required, and whether a site visit is necessary before submitting the response.

RESPONDING TO RFQS AND RFPS

Preparing a compelling and competitive proposal is crucial for success in government contracting. Doing so is not a template-based or cookie-cutter process and should not be considered such. While all will follow the same basic format and are governed by the same or similar regulations, each RFP is entirely different from any other. Each opportunity has been created by a different agency, written by different people, requesting different products or services.

Businesses who want to create an effective response to the opportunity should treat each as unique.

Initially, a thorough reading and review of all documents is necessary. It may be required to read some sections multiple times and highlight areas or take specific notes regarding pertinent information so that a business can ensure compliance with any special instructions and clearly understand what is required in the offer. Reading the specific evaluation criteria will allow the company to customize its proposal to address the agency's particular needs and preferences, whether highlighting relevant experience and qualifications or notating technical expertise regarding a product or service.

Crafting a competitive proposal begins with a complete understanding of what the agency wants, how they want it delivered, and creating a response that shows how that is best accomplished. Avoiding "boilerplate" response templates when responding to RFPs is best. While this is the easy way to create proposals, a business sacrifices any competitive edge they may possess by taking this route.

Understanding the framework of RFPs is essential for navigating the world of government contracting. Being familiar with these documents' structure, purpose, and significance can help a contractor effectively respond to procurement opportunities and best position themselves for success. Adhering to best practices and submitting proposals demonstrating value, compliance, and technical competence increase a contractor's chance of winning more and potentially higher-value government contracts.

CHAPTER HIGHLIGHTS

1. Understanding the core components of an RFP is crucial to creating successful responses and winning more contracts.

2. Compliance with regulations, guidelines, response format, evaluation criteria, and every other aspect of an RFP is crucial. "Compliance" can often be translated as "following instructions."

ACTION STEPS

1. Read, read, then read again each and every RFP prior to beginning the response process.

2. Study the evaluation criteria closely and customize any responses to the wants and needs of the posting agency so as to maximize chances for success.

CHAPTER 8

TURNING KNOWLEDGE INTO SUCCESS

In the world of business, government contracting presents a unique and potentially lucrative opportunity. The journey through understanding and navigating this sector can be complex, but with the insights from the previous chapters of this book, a business diving into the world of government contracting is now equipped with the knowledge needed to embark on this path confidently. This final chapter aims to weave together the lessons learned into a cohesive, actionable strategy that can propel a company toward success in government contracting. Here are some insights from "Government Contracting Unveiled" through "Understanding RFPs" into practical steps that can be followed easily.

ESTABLISHING THE FOUNDATION

The first crucial action is ensuring the business is properly registered and meets all qualifications for government contracting. As discussed in the chapters on federal and state/local registration, getting a business registered on the System for Award Management (SAM) and obtaining any necessary small business certifications are foundational steps. These certifications can significantly enhance a competitive edge by qualifying the business for set-aside contracts. Start by meticulously reviewing the registration details and certifications to ensure accuracy and completeness, as these are key to opening doors in the government marketplace.

IDENTIFYING OPPORTUNITIES

With the foundation set, the next step involves identifying potential contracting opportunities. Utilize the resources and strategies outlined in the chapters on federal and state/local opportunities. A business should regularly browse through SAM, FedBizOpps, and local government portals to find opportunities that match the business's capabilities and expertise. This proactive approach is vital in spotting the right opportunities early and preparing bids or proposals with sufficient time.

MASTERING THE PROCUREMENT PROCESS

Understanding the procurement methods governments use, such as RFPs, RFQs, and BPAs, is crucial. Each method has its nuances and requirements, as highlighted in the relevant chapter. Tailored approaches based on the specific procurement method increase the chances for success immensely. For RFPs, focus on crafting detailed proposals that clearly demonstrate how the business can meet the government's needs. For RFQs, emphasize a product or service's value and cost-effectiveness. And for BPAs understand that building a relationship based on reliability and quality can lead to ongoing opportunities.

CRAFTING WINNING PROPOSALS

A significant portion of the success in government contracting will hinge on a company's ability to respond effectively to RFPs. The chapter on understanding RFPs provides a wealth of knowledge on interpreting these documents and crafting compelling proposals. Pay close attention to the evaluation criteria mentioned in RFPs and ensure the proposal addresses each point concisely. Highlighting the business's unique strengths and how they align with the government's requirements can set a proposal apart.

LEVERAGING RELATIONSHIPS AND NETWORKING

Building relationships with government officials and other contractors is an invaluable strategy that extends beyond the paperwork. Attend government-hosted events, industry days, and other networking functions to get the business's name out there. These interactions can lead to partnerships, subcontracting opportunities, and valuable insights into upcoming projects. Remember, the government contracting world thrives on trust and reliability, so establishing and maintaining positive relationships is key.

CONTINUOUS LEARNING AND ADAPTATION

The government contracting landscape is always evolving. Laws change, new technologies emerge, and market demands shift. A business must stay informed about these changes by attending workshops, webinars, and courses on government contracting. Engage with contracting officers to receive feedback on bids, regardless of the outcome. This continuous learning mindset will help refine the approach, improve the proposals, and stay competitive.

PERSISTENCE AND RESILIENCE

Perhaps the most important lesson is the value of persistence and resilience. Success in government contracting rarely happens overnight. It requires dedication, hard work, and the ability to learn from setbacks. Each proposal, whether successful or not, provides a learning opportunity. Embrace these experiences, refine strategies, and remain steadfast in the pursuit.

EMBARKING ON YOUR JOURNEY

Wrapping up this journey through the world of government contracting, remember that the key to success lies in taking informed, deliberate actions. By establishing a solid foundation, identifying and pursuing the right opportunities, mastering the procurement process, crafting winning proposals, building strong relationships, continuously learning, and staying persistent, a company can navigate the complexities of government contracting with confidence.

This chapter is not the end but a new beginning. Armed with the knowledge from this book and a positive, action-oriented mindset, businesses are well-prepared to embark on a successful journey in government contracting. Remember, every step taken is a move towards achieving the business goals in this challenging yet rewarding field. Keep pushing forward, stay adaptable, and let the business's strengths shine through in every proposal and interaction. The world of government contracting is vast and full of opportunities—the next successful contract could be just around the corner.

APPENDIX A

TAA Qualifying Countries
(as of November 2023)

Afghanistan	France	Niger
Angola	Gambia	North Macedonia
Antigua & Barbuda	Germany	Norway
Armenia	Greece	Oman
Aruba	Grenada	Panama
Australia	Guatemala	Peru
Austria	Guinea	Poland
Bahamas	Guinea-Bissau	Portugal
Bahrain	Guyana	Romania

Bangladesh	Haiti	Rwanda
Barbados	Honduras	Saba
Belgium	Hong Kong	Samoa
Belize	Hungary	Sao Tome & Principe
Benin	Iceland	Senegal
Bhutan	Ireland	Sierra Leone
Bonaire	Israel	Singapore
British Virgin Islands	Italy	Sint Eustatius
Bulgaria	Jamaica	Sint Maarten
Burkina Faso	Japan	Slovak Republic
Burundi	Kiribati	Slovenia
Cambodia	Korea (Republic of)	Solomon Islands
Canada	Laos	Somalia

Central African Republic	Latvia	South Sudan
Chad	Lesotho	Spain
Chile	Liberia	St. Kitts & Nevis
Colombia	Liechtenstein	St. Lucia
Comoros	Lithuania	St. Vincent & the Grenadines
Costa Rica	Luxembourg	Sweden
Croatia	Madagascar	Switzerland
Curacao	Malawi	Taiwan
Cyprus	Mali	Tanzania
Czech Republic	Malta	Timor-Leste
Democratic Republic of Congo	Mauritania	Togo
Denmark	Mexico	Trinidad & Tobago

Djibouti	Moldova	Tuvalu
Dominica	Montenegro	Uganda
Dominican Republic	Montserrat	Ukraine
El Salvador	Morocco	United Kingdom
Equatorial Guinea	Mozambique	Vanuatu
Eritrea	Nepal	Yemen
Estonia	Netherlands	Zambia
Ethiopia	New Zealand	
Finland	Nicaragua